Going to the UK?

Ten Things You Should Know

By Rajiv Immanuel

ISBN-13: 978-1502333629

ISBN-10: 1502333627

Note from the Author

In this book, the words "UK" and "Britain" are used interchangeably to mean the same place. Where the information refers to England only and not to the rest of the UK (Wales, Scotland and Northern Ireland) that is indicated separately. The last UK Census was held in 2011. Data in this book that draws from the Census is therefore from 2011.

The material in this book is for general information only and does not constitute investment, tax, legal, career, financial, immigration or other form of advice. You should not rely on this information to make (or refrain from making) any decisions. Links to external sites are for information only and do not constitute endorsement. Always obtain independent, professional advice for your own particular situation.

List of Important UK Phone Numbers

Police/Fire/Ambulance (emergency): 999

Police (non-emergency): 101

NHS Direct (free medical advice): 111

British Transport Police: 0800 40 50 40

Renting charity Shelter helpline: 0808 8004444

For London bus arrival info (chargeable): send bus-stop code by text to 87287

Contents

Introduction

The UK is a fantastic country to live, work or study in. It is a land of promise and opportunity and the UK needs you if you have good written and spoken English, are young, skilled, hard-working, ambitious, and willing to learn and adapt.

In the UK there are tremendous potential opportunities for people who are young, skilled and hardworking.

Are you are keen to move to the UK to live, work or study? If so, your mind may be full of questions about various aspects of UK life.

The author too was in that position nearly twenty years ago.

He arrived in the UK as an international student in 1995. Since then he has worked in the UK, seen success and failure, interacted closely with the British, and knows the good and bad about this country. He is now a professional watcher of Britain and a writer of books preparing others for UK life.

In this book, he distils his nearly two decades of experience of living in the UK to give you ten important tips about UK life.

This book warns you of the mistakes that you should not make while living in the UK.

Your UK life should be a positive and life-changing experience, bringing new qualifications, a new career, financial security, growth and opportunities.

It should not be a humiliating, unhappy or tragic experience.

"We sent our son to the UK to study so that he could have a better life. We never thought he would be in any danger. The way in which he was taken from us is absolutely devastating." This was the reaction of Thavisha Peiris' parents in Sri Lanka on their son's murder in Sheffield, UK. Be warned there are dangers lurking in Britain. Britain can be a safe place. But you must not be naive and base your life and actions on wrong notions. Learn from one who has been an observer of this country for two decades. This book is more than mere information. This is advice based on experience.

The author, Rajiv Immanuel, tells you about life in the UK as it actually is, with no attempt to be economical with the truth. Saving your life and ensuring your UK mission is a success is the goal of this book. Don't waste your time in the UK going round in circles making mistakes that could even cost you your life. Let your UK life begin on a positive note with the tips in this book.

FREE: As a bonus, the author is giving away his book Best UK Jobs for Foreigners: Jobs with less competition from Britons (worth $2.99) free within this book. Yes, two books for the price of one. The free book is included in this book.

Chapter 1. Don't Lose Your Life in the UK!

You could be forgiven for thinking that the UK is a safe place for foreigners to live, work or study. Like the foreigners mentioned in this book, I too, a newly arrived foreigner in the UK, thought so.

I too thought that the UK would be a much safer place than where I came from: India. That was in 1995. All these cases mentioned in this book occurred since then. I am now older and wiser. You must be warned that there are dangers lurking in Britain. Britain can be a safe place. But you must not be naive and base your life and actions on wrong notions.

Base your life on realities which this book will tell you about. You owe it to yourself, your family and all those who are concerned about your welfare to take care of yourself while in the UK. This book will show you how.

The UK is generally a safe place if you take certain precautions mentioned in this book. The objective of this book is to ensure that no other foreigner faces the same fate that befell these unfortunate young people whose stories are told below.

Amelie Delagrange

According to her parents, Amelie Delagrange, 22, from Amiens in France had a passion for the English language and had moved to Britain to further her studies.

She was living in Twickenham, south-west London. She enjoyed living in the UK. She had been living in London for just three months when she was killed.

Her parents Jean Francois and Dominique Delagrange travelled from France to the Old Bailey (Court) to hear the details of their daughter's death.

"She was a good student, sensible, and never gave her parents any problems," her mother told the court.

Her boyfriend, Olivier Lenfant, also described her as a sensible girl who thought she lived in a safe area.

In a statement in 2008 Ms Delagrange's parents said: "It is nearly four years since our lives and our family's lives were so seriously disrupted, descending into a horror - a living nightmare."

It was August 2004, Amelie was returning home by bus at about 10 pm. On the way, she missed her bus stop and decided to get down at the next stop after asking the bus driver for directions. She then began walking back towards her home and took a short cut through Twickenham Green, where she was assaulted by Levi Bellfield, sustaining a severe head injury.

She died in hospital from her injuries that night. A post-mortem examination revealed her injuries had been caused by an object similar to a hammer or a crowbar.

Levi Bellfield (39 at the time) her killer was a former nightclub bouncer. He was convicted in February 2008 of murdering not only Amelie Delagrange but also Marsha McDonnell, and Milly Dowler. Additionally, he was convicted of the attempted murder of Kate Sheedy. In June 2011, Bellfield was sentenced to life imprisonment.

During his trial at the Old Bailey in London the prosecution said Bellfield trawled buses and bus stops for women and attacked them when they rejected him.

Thavisha Peiris

South Yorkshire Police said that the night of 27 October 2013 was a particularly dark, wet, and cold one. The tragedy happened in a dimly lit area in Sheffield, a city known for high crime levels.

Thavisha Peiris arrived at about 10 pm to deliver a pizza for Domino's Pizza. His friends would later describe him as a very generous person, friendly, talkative and fun

Thavisha Peiris had only been in the UK for two years, and was due to start a new career in IT. The 25-year-old former Sheffield Hallam University student from Sri Lanka was planning to go into business with three friends.

His dreams ended tragically. He was stabbed to death in a "frenzied" knife attack on his final shift as a pizza delivery driver. His colleague found him dead in the driving seat of his Toyota Yaris, parked near where he was due to make a delivery in Sheffield.

He was the youngest in a large family from Colombo, Sri Lanka. His parents paid for his studies using their own retirement money. He came to the UK with high hopes and aspirations.

His studies went well. He completed a degree in Information Technology. To pay his bills, he secured a part-time delivery job at Domino's Pizza.

Mr Peiris bled to death following a violent knife attack by Kasim Ahmed, 18, and Shamraze Khan, 26, who tried to steal his mobile phone.

A post-mortem examination revealed he had suffered 14 stab wounds, including one which severed his carotid artery and another to his heart.

They were jailed for a minimum of 23 and 24 years respectively.

His parents Sarath Peiris and Sudharma Narangoda had said they thought Britain was a "safe" place for their son to study. They had wanted the best for their son.

His parents told the BBC: "All we have left are our memories, but they will never fill the void in our hearts. He will never again be with us and we will never hear his voice again."

Det Supt of the Police Lisa Ray described the case as "the saddest case" she had dealt with

In a statement Thavisha's parents said: "We are still devastated and heartbroken over the loss of Thavisha and we are still unable to comprehend that he is actually gone."

Sukhwinder Singh

In January 2010, a 31-year-old builder, Sukhwinder Singh, was stabbed to death after he chased two men who had mugged a woman in Barking, East London.

His murder remains unsolved despite police offering a £20,000 reward.

Mr Singh died at the Royal London Hospital. A post mortem test showed he died from a stab wound to the heart.

Barking councillor Nirmal Singh Gill said: "He would help anybody so it doesn't surprise me he was trying to help a lady. He didn't deserve this - but he was a special young man. It's a very big loss to everyone both here and in India."

Police said father-of-one Mr Singh was an Indian national who had lived in the UK for about 10 years.

The two suspects were described as black, aged in their 20s to 30s, and both were about 5ft 7in to 6ft.

Police said: "What Mr Singh did was very brave. I would not encourage people to get involved, I'd encourage people to call 999 so the police can respond.

Sir Paul Stephenson, London Metropolitan police commissioner said "In an increasingly violent society there is more likelihood that members of the public who intervene will be shot or maimed."

In England and Wales, anyone can use "reasonable" force to protect themselves or others, or to carry out an arrest or to prevent crime.

According to the UK Home Office: "As long as they use no more force than necessary, people should have confidence that the law will support them."

British culture, however, does not support intervention in crimes. Research has shown that six out of 10 Britons would be unlikely to challenge a group of 14-year-old boys vandalising a bus shelter. This was the highest in Europe - more than Germany, the Netherlands, Italy, France and Spain.

Anuj Bidve

Anuj Bidve, 23, was from Pune, in India. He had graduated in engineering from the University of Pune in India.

His family said he had chosen to study in the UK because they thought it would be a safe place to study.

He was studying for a masters degree in microelectronics at Lancaster University.

Kiaran Stapleton, 22, was the fourth of nine children. He was an anxious child whose behaviour had deteriorated at secondary school. He was excluded from school aged 14 more than once for fighting.

He is currently serving life in prison for murdering Indian student Anuj Bidve.

Kiaran Stapleton shot dead Anuj as he walked to the Manchester sales with friends on 26 December, 2011.

The university's vice chancellor Professor Mark Smith said at the graduation ceremony, "This terrible event highlights the vagaries of the world, and indeed life, and how in one moment your life can change."

Mr Bidve had only been in the country for three months when he was killed.

Kiaran Stapleton, 21, was found guilty of murder at Manchester Crown Court on Thursday following a five-week trial. Stapleton was told he would serve a minimum term of 30 years.

During his first appearance before magistrates, Stapleton was asked if his name was Kiaran Stapleton. He replied: "No, Psycho. Psycho Stapleton."

His trial heard that both prosecution and defence agreed he had a recognised medical condition of anti-social personality disorder and that he had psychopathic traits.

The Judge Mr Justice King said Stapleton had committed a "truly wicked act" and was a "highly dangerous man" who posed a high risk of serious harm to other people. He told Stapleton: "In my judgment, this was no impulsive act on your part. It was a piece of cold-blooded controlled aggression. When you went out you were fully minded to find a victim to satisfy your desire to shoot and kill someone if you could. By that single act of cruelty you brought about the premature death of a bright young man who had already achieved so much and had so much to look forward to in the future. He said he had showed a "most callous disregard" in laughing and smirking after he gunned down Mr Bidve and also during the trial."

"You have behaved in a way demonstrating that you are positively boastful about having killed Mr Bidve," the Judge said.

Anuj and his friends left their hotel in Salford to queue early for the Boxing Day sales to try to grab any bargains. Unfortunately for them, they came across Stapleton and his friend who asked them for the time. He then pulled a handgun out of his pocket and fired one shot to Anuj Bidve's left temple.

Asked during the trial why he had shot a complete stranger, he answered: "I honestly don't know."

Piotr Mikiewicz

Piotr Mikiewicz, 40 from Poland was a street cleaner in west London. In August 2012 Mr Mikiewicz hit Roger Buckingham, 31, a burglar, with his broom after seeing him coming out of a house in Shepher's Bush where a burglar alarm was sounding.

Mr Mikiewicz had started hitting him with the broom to try to stop him.

Roger Buckingham, stabbed Mr Mikiewicz in the chest, and the latter died. Buckingham was jailed for a minimum of 27 years.

The killer had 25 previous convictions for 51 offences.

The Recorder of London, Judge Brian Barker, said of Piotr: "He was a brave man who acted beyond the call of duty."

"He ignored his own safety and he paid for his actions with his life."

Piotr's wife said: "Anyone who knew Piotr knew he was a truly good and honest person. He had a strong sense of what was right and wrong."

"He wasn't just a road sweeper, he was part of the community that genuinely cared for him."

"A cruel and thoughtless act can take away his life, but not the inspiration that he brought to so many people."

The judge said Buckingham had acted "in frustration and temper," and added: "On any view, it was cowardly and selfish."

Damilola Taylor

Damilola Taylor was a 10-year old boy from Nigeria. In the summer of 2000, Damilola's family moved from Nigeria to Peckham, London in search of a better life. On 27 November of that year as he walked home from school he was stabbed in the leg with broken glass by two brothers, Danny and Ricky Preddie, who were persistent young offenders. He bled to death. It took six years and three trials to identify and convict his killers. He died in a concrete stairwell, on a condemned housing estate, a few hundred yards from the safety of his home. He wanted to be a doctor. He was only in the UK for a few months but all his dreams were destroyed at such a young age.

Council housing is cheap government housing let out by the local government authority. It is designed for the very poor and socially disadvantaged classes (single mums, ex-offenders, homeless people etc). Council estates, especially in London, can be dangerous places because of gangs, drugs, drug dealers, knives and guns.

During 2007-2013, 124 teenagers were murdered in London, mainly due to gang-related violence. A knife crime happens every 50 minutes in London. Areas around council estates are where many of these crimes happen. (Source: www.citizensreport.org)

The killers of British army drummer Lee Rigby (murdered in May 2013) lived on a council estate in Greenwich. They were involved in gang wars. Their parents had lost control over them. They fell under the sway of extremists.

Newly arrived foreigners are very vulnerable in the UK:

Francisco Hounye

American student Francesco Hounye (22) from Florida, suffered severe facial injuries after being hit with a bottle near Brick Lane (a street in East London, in the London Borough of Tower Hamlets) on June 17, 2013.

The assault by a gang happened at 12:20 am. He had only been in the UK for three days when he was attacked. He and his friend tried to escape but the gang chased them. Police said: "He had come to the UK to enhance his studies and has been left so shocked and horrified by what happened that he feels unsafe and is unsure if he wants to stay here."

Mr.Hounye was attacked by a group of five Asian men who also kicked and punched him. He suffered permanent scarring and a chipped tooth. Mr Hounye said: "Every time I look in the mirror from now on I will be reminded of this incident." Mr.Hounye had been out in the Brick Lane area of London with a friend at midnight.

London's Metropolitan Police said they believed Mr Hounye had been targeted because he was "obviously not local" and answered back. It could also be because he was drinking alcohol in Brick Lane, a part of London dominated by Muslim residents. He was taken to the Royal London Hospital with deep slash wounds to his head, which required 23 stitches to his face and more stitches internally.

Mr Hounye said: "As a result of this incident I am now scared to go out on my own in London. I feel very emotional about the whole situation. I also now face the rest of my life with the permanent scarring that will be left on my face as a result of this attack."

Joao Esteves

Joao Esteves, 45, from Lisbon, Portugal had been in the UK for less than a week when he was found with head injuries in Crawley on 19 January 2014. After failing to find work he was trying to return home to Portugal. Mr Esteves had approached the Crawley Open House shelter for the homeless but they had no room. He was advised to sleep outside until the morning, according to information revealed in court.

The court heard that on the night of Mr Esteves' death, Palmer had drunk about eight pints of beer, had threatened to punch one man, and was thrown out of a bar in Crawley after getting into a fight with another. A video and a number of photographs of the victim lying unconscious were found on Palmer's mobile phone, the court was told. Daniel Palmer, 24, from Station Hill, Crawley, was jailed for life and ordered to serve a minimum of 15 years. Police said Palmer filmed his victim after the attack and sent the footage to friends "almost as a trophy."

Det Ch Insp Jason Taylor said: "He refused to answer questions about the attack but we were able to prove with CCTV, DNA evidence and witnesses that he caused Mr. Esteves' terrible injuries."

London's gang culture: The story of Learco Chindamo

The story of Learco Chindamo exemplifies London's gang culture and its dangers. Learco Chindamo murdered secondary school headmaster Philip Lawrence outside his north London school in 1995. Learco was only 15-years-old at that time.

Chindamo's involvement with London's gang culture began early. He was born in Milan in 1980 to an Italian father and Filipino mother. He moved to London aged six with his mother and two brothers, two years after the breakdown of his parents' relationship.

He stopped going to school. He spent much time with a gang which roamed the streets and shopping malls of west London. He was an immature kid trying to act grown up, intimidating people with his like-minded knife-carrying fellow gang members. They were completely out of control. The murder he committed saved the public from further trouble from him for a while. He spent about 12 years in prison.

Is Britain a safe country?

Yes, it is, if you take certain precautions.

Be on your guard if you live in a town known for crime. Many parts of the UK suffer from high crime rates. Many towns and cities in the UK have streets where criminal gangs operate, selling and taking drugs, drinking, vandalising cars and property.

Towns/parts of the UK known for anti-social behaviour:

Corby (Northamptonshire)

Mansfield (Nottinghamshire)

Hackney (London)

Nottingham

Luton (Bedfordshire)

Slough (Berkshire)

Ashfield (Nottinghamshire)

Knowsley (Merseyside)

Middlesborough (Cleveland)

Easington (County Durham)

For a more detailed look at the subject of avoiding crime in the UK please refer to the author's book *Complete Guide to Living, Working and Studying in the UK: Preparing You for Life in Britain* available at Amazon.

Remember, you are vulnerable as a new arrival in the UK. Mr Bidve had only been in the country for three months when he was killed. Mr.Hounye had only been in the UK for three days.

Don't be out and about in the middle of the night. Anuj Bidve and his friends had left their hotel to join sales queues at 00:45 GMT. Amelie de la Grange was killed at 10pm when she was walking home. Francisco Hounye was attacked at 12:20 am. Being out in the middle of the night is courting disaster.

Being out late at night in city centres/roads can be very dangerous for anyone not only foreigners. Do not engage with yobs (antisocial youth). A BBC presenter Nicky Campbell was spat upon and verbally abused after he confronted yobs ripping open bin bags and kicking rubbish in Clapham, south London in 2011. Mr.Anuj Bidve did not consider that he might encounter a gun-carrying youth in a British town centre. Did Mr.Peiris or his family know that Sheffield is a place listed in the top ten for high levels of crime and burglary in the UK? These were recipes for disaster. And disaster happened.

Don't be a have a go hero. Call the police instead on 999. Mr.Sukhwinder Singh and Mr.Mickwiecz quite forgot that this was London, and were all-alone dealing with knife-wielding thugs. Did they know that a knife crime happens every 50 minutes in London?

It can be dangerous to live in or around council estates in London, and you must keep track of your children at all times.

Chapter 2. Britain is a Highly Regulated Society

Newly arrived foreigners in the UK are very vulnerable not only as victims of crime but also as law-breakers themselves. Do not be ignorant of the law.

Be aware of the law

A good thing about the UK is that there is no arbitrariness from UK public bodies. People cannot operate on their own interpretations of the law. You cannot bribe public officials and flout the law. There are laws or rules about everything and rules are enforced in the UK.

You could pay £80 for doing the following in the street:

- Spitting in the street
- Dropping a bank card
- Dropping nut shells
- Dropping orange peel
- Dropping a pen
- Dropping a banana skin
- Dropping a cigarette butt
- Feeding pigeons

You can be fined by the local council if you put rubbish in the wrong bin or if you overfill your rubbish/recycling bin.

Even personal trainers who train clients to be fit in public parks, can be forced to pay up to £600 a year to use public parks in London, while professional dog walkers also need to pay £300 a year plus VAT to use public parks. The idea is that commercial activity in public places needs to have a licence.

Posting offensive messages on social media, Facebook or Twitter

After the England riots of 2011, two people were jailed for their posts on social networking sites despite the fact no trouble was reported in either area.

Jordan Blackshaw, 21, created a Facebook event entitled "Smash d[o]wn in Northwich Town. Perry Sutcliffe-Keenan, 22, invited people to "riot" in Warrington on 10 August.

Both men pleaded guilty under sections 44 and 46 of the Serious Crime Act to intentionally encouraging another to assist the commission of an indictable offence. They were jailed for four years each.

Peter Copeland, 29, a Sunderland football club fan, received a four-month suspended jail sentence after he posted racist comments aimed at Newcastle United fans, under the Malicious Communications Act.

Joshua Cryer, 21, admitting bombarding former footballer Stan Collymore with a series of racist tweets in an attempt to "snare a celebrity" by provoking a reaction. He was charged under section 127 of the Communications Act with sending grossly offensive messages and given a two-year community order.

Liam Stacey, a student who made racially offensive comments about footballer Fabrice Muamba on Twitter was jailed for 56 days after he admitted a racially aggravated public order offence.

A lady driver was convicted of driving offences after tweeting about a collision with a cyclist. Emma Way, 22, from Norfolk, was found guilty at Norwich Magistrates' Court of failing to stop after a collision and failing to report an accident.

She tweeted "definitely knocked a cyclist off his bike earlier. I have right of way - he doesn't even pay road tax!" using the hashtag #bloodycyclists. Cyclist Toby Hockley, from Norwich, suffered bruising and minor damage to his bike in the incident in Norfolk.

A total of 653 people faced criminal charges in England and Wales in 2012 in connection with comments on Twitter or Facebook.

Driving offences that put points on your licence

- Speeding – 3-6 points

- Using a hand-held mobile phone while driving - 3 points

- Driving through a red light - 3 points

- Racing other cars on public roads – 3-11 points

- Driving an uninsured vehicle – 6-8 points

- Driving while unfit due to drink (whether or not over the legal alcohol limit) -10 points

Note: A fine may be imposed along with points on your licence. Having 12 or more points on your licence triggers an automatic driving ban.

Other driving offences that could invite fines or points or both:

- Lane hogging on motorways (driving continuously in the middle/outside lane of a motorway)

- Mounting a kerb

- Driving fast through puddles

- Driving too close to the vehicle in front

- Failing to give way at a junction

- Overtaking and pushing into a queue of traffic

- Spinning wheels unnecessarily

- Doing a hand-brake turn

- Driver taking photographs of an accident site on roads while driving past

Offences that might be overlooked in another country are not overlooked here.

A woman who shouted racist abuse on a train at fellow non-white passengers was given a 24 month community order.

A man from Warrington was given a suspended jail sentence after his Staffordshire bull terrier decapitated a smaller dog.

A biker who performed a wheelie at 110mph in a 70mph zone was banned from driving. He was disqualified from driving for 20 months and given a 12-week prison sentence suspended for two years. Police said he had shown a "complete contempt for motoring laws."

Few get away by breaking the law in the UK. It is not a lawless society. Whenever lawlessness occurs, it is dealt with firmly. After the England riots of 2011, tough sentences were handed out to the criminals who indulged in looting/stealing/antisocial behaviour. During the rioting, a man who stole a mineral water bottle from Lidl costing £3.50 was jailed for six months.

The government is not far behind criminals. Legislation constantly moves to keep pace with change. In 2013, the Association of Chief Police Officers (Acpo) estimated that the illegal trade in stolen metal in the UK was costing the UK economy £770 million a year. The illegal trade affected the rail and power industries and churches were targeted for lead. The government moved quickly to enact The Scrap Metal Dealers Act 2013 - a new law targeting trade in stolen metal. All scrap dealers and motor salvage operators in England and Wales are now required to apply for a licence from their local authority and keep records on who they buy from. A ban was introduced on cash payments to mobile collectors. The idea was to make it easier to trace people selling stolen metal.

A Pakistani airline pilot was jailed for nine months for being drunk in his cockpit before a flight. The judge said it was "astonishing that foreign pilots flying out of UK airports were unaware of the law here and believed it was legal to fly if there was a 12 hour gap between drinking and flying."

Captain Irfan Faiz, 55, was more than four times the drink-fly limit when he was breathalysed after being spotted 'staggering' and 'not walking straight' on the way to the plane, a court heard.

He was arrested and taken to a police station for questioning. Moments earlier he had been doing pre-flight checks in an Airbus aircraft, which was due to fly from Leeds-Bradford airport to Islamabad in Pakistan with 145 passengers and 11 crew on board. An initial breath test showed he had 41 microgrammes of alcohol in 100 millilitres of breath (the limit for driving is 35 and for flying is 9). Faiz's solicitor told the court his client 'had no idea' he was breaking UK rules at the time of the incident in September.

An Iranian-born property developer, Hekmat Kaveh (55) the owner of one of Britain's top independent schools was ordered to pay nearly £50,000 for risking pupils' lives by having 'woefully inadequate' fire safety measures. Kaveh, who runs The Abbey College in Malvern, Worcestershire, admitted 15 fire safety breaches. Worcester Crown Court heard the school, which had around 200 pupils aged 14-20 on the rolls, had 'defective smoke alarms and non-functional fire doors in student sleeping areas.'

Four members of Sri Lanka's Commonwealth Games team were stopped by police when they were spotted cycling down the M74 near Glasgow in July 2014. They were seen on one of Scotland's busiest roads. Police told them they were breaking the law - cycling on motorways is banned by law. A similar incident happened during the 2002 Games in Manchester when two cyclists from Kenya travelled 17 miles down the M61 before being stopped by police near Bolton.

Three hundred Libyan soldiers were undergoing training at Cambridgeshire's Bassingbourn Barracks under plans by the UK Government to train up to 2,000 cadets to ensure Libya's transition to democracy and its security. The armed forces personnel arrived at the barracks from Libya in June 2014 for training in basic infantry skills and junior leadership skills. Three soldiers were detained by Cambridgeshire Police in October 2014 (just four months later) in connection with "offences relating to incidents in Cambridge." All three were charged with sexually assaulting women. Two of them pleaded guilty. One of them was also charged with indecent exposure and stealing a bicycle. One also admitted using threatening behaviour towards a police officer. All three were remanded in custody.

The UK is a highly regulated society that takes its legislation seriously. Find out the legislation affecting your field of work. Avoid a criminal conviction and fines/prison. Find out what is and isn't a criminal offence in the UK. Find out the legislation affecting your field of work. These and related questions are answered in detail in the author's book *Complete Guide to Living, Working and Studying in the UK: Preparing You for Life in Britain (available on Amazon).*

Chapter 3. Language and Etiquette

The importance of learning English

The British do not take foreigners seriously who are not good at English. You therefore need good English, both written and spoken. Foreign accents need modification. If you do have a foreign accent, speak slowly and clearly, enunciating the words with care.

In any job interview, the British would tend to prefer foreigners who speak and write good English. They love those who love their language. Foreigners who don't get jobs, because of poor English or no local qualifications, tend to run restaurants, corner shops, newsagents, taxis, and post offices or non-supermarket petrol stations or fruit/vegetable picking and packing. The only option for those lacking English is to do low-paid menial jobs like cleaning, cutting salads for supermarkets or stocking shelves at night for supermarkets.

The British authorities are tightening the screws on foreign staff whose English is not up to the mark The Nursing and Midwifery Council has asked the government for the right to test the English language skills of applicants from within the EU in the same way they test applicants from outside Europe.

Even doctors' English skills are under scrutiny. New powers to test doctors' language skills could be introduced in the UK after a survey showed that patients' lives were being put at risk.

A tragic incident brought foreign doctors'English skills into the spotlight. In 2008, Nigerian-born Dr Daniel Ubani, a locum (temporary) doctor came to the UK from Germany to see a patient. He was working for a firm providing locum doctors for the NHS.

He killed David Gray with 10 times the recommended dose of diamorphine after confusing it with another drug on his first and only shift in the UK. He had earlier been rejected for work because of poor English skills.

An alarming 66 cases were investigated by senior NHS staff in 2011 after patients complained that they had received poor treatment from doctors who had a poor grasp of English. This applies to both EU and non-EU doctors.

The government is also concerned about the English language skills of carers. About 20% of carers in the UK are from abroad. 2011 census figures showed that across England 1.7 per cent of the population - more than a million people - have either no, or poor spoken English. That figure rises to 9 per cent in some London boroughs where about 30% of the population is born abroad. UK Communities Secretary Eric Pickles has warned that those who fail to speak English 'are condemned to a limited life'.

Mr Pickles said, 'Speaking English is crucial to allow us to come together and be part of British society. People are unable to do this and are condemned to a limited life if they can't speak our language.

'To be a proper functioning citizen you must be able to speak English. Those who can't are missing out much of British society, such as participating in civic life, talking to neighbours, or popping to the shops.

Foreigners who desire to fulfil their potential, communicate with friends, neighbours and colleagues, have better-paid employment and increased self-confidence have to speak and write excellent English.

Learn British Etiquette

Britain has for long set the standards for etiquette and good taste in the world. Those who train butlers for a living suggest that this is because Britain has a history of the class system, of household staff, of etiquette, and great traditions. They argue that when it comes to training household staff, of any nationality, rich clients, particularly in the Middle East, value the British style.

Remember, you don't have to use 'Sir' or 'Madam' when you address people. You can call virtually anyone by their first name, even your professor, tutor, supervisor. Do not use 'Sir' or 'Madam'. By doing so you advertise that you are from a different culture/foreign country. Don't call a driver 'Driver', or a waiter a 'Waiter'. This demeans them. In traditional societies this may be ok, but not in Britain. Avoid using any title. Just say what you want without a prefix. Add the suffix "please." And remember to say "Thank you."

British etiquette points to remember

• Always queue.

• Never answer a mobile phone during a meal or a business meeting.

• Always hold a door open for someone regardless of who they are.

• At the dining table, do not drink from cans/bottles. Use a glass.

• Do not criticise Britain.

• The large spoon at the top of your plate is for dessert. Do not use it to eat the meal.

• Do not confuse the tiny milk jug (it is for tea/coffee) for the larger cream jug (it is for pouring on desserts).

• Talk quietly in public, especially if you are speaking a foreign language.

• Eat quietly. Avoid chewing noises.

• Do not ask personal questions.

• Do not forget to say 'please' and 'thank you.'

Keeping up Appearances

The sitcom Keeping up Appearances was a 1980s/90s British comedy about a British lady, Hyacinth, obsessed with outward appearances, and the importance of giving the right impression. Even though a comedy, the programme highlighted an important reality: that there is truth in the idea that giving the right impression is fundamental to getting anywhere in Britain.

Take the following example: a brilliant accountant from overseas, known to the author, did not get a top job. She was told later when she asked the interview committee for feedback: "The interview board felt that you were easily the best candidate at the interview. However, when you had the discussion part of the selection (with future colleagues), you spoke too loudly, and they were put off. We had to appoint the next preferred candidate" (author's note: candidate no.2 was a local person). Be aware that British candidates at interviews may use their cultural familiarity with the selectors to their advantage, as indicated here.

Avoid a foreign sounding name, you could face racism. There have been many instances where recruiters have been known to avoid calling those candidates for interview who have an obviously foreign name. Change/abbreviate your name to something with three or four letters which the Brits can understand. The Brits love one syllable first names. Your new first name should also be a valid English name for e.g.:

Vic

Rod

Sam

Ash

Kris

Pam

Pat

Bob

Sue

Tony

Dave

Dan

Chris...

Remember, there is no legal requirement to use your given name. You can use any name for daily living. You can change your real name by a process known as "Deed Poll."

In some societies, it may not be considered impolite to eat noisily. But in Britain it is a hallmark of bad manners. Eat food without making chomping noises. Do not express excessive interest in the food when eating socially. Try not to handle the food, use the fork and knife instead.

For ladies, have your hair cut professionally or the Brits will laugh at you behind your back. There are always women hairdressers who will call on you at home and cut your hair for a lot less than the high street salon. Check the Yellow Pages for such things.

Regarding dealing with the opposite sex, in other societies, it may be ok to praise a colleague's clothing or put your arm around an office colleague. You may think it is a friendly gesture or a compliment. But in Britain, flirtatious behaviour in the office could be deemed as sexual harassment. The key point to ask yourself is: is the behaviour intimidating, offensive, degrading or humiliating?

Chapter 4. Making Progress in Your Career

How to get a job easily

Point one: While some European, American, Australian and New Zealand professional qualifications are acceptable in the UK, particularly in teaching, in general however, UK employers do not care much for foreign qualifications.

Point two: The UK has an oversupply of low-skilled workers, for whom demand is falling, according to the European Union Council in 2012. This is bad news for low-skilled immigrants because this affects their job prospects. This means that low-skilled immigrants may have to copy the early Asian immigrants to the UK in the 1960s and 1970s who drove buses, started curry houses and ran corner shops. Unless you possess skills highly demanded by the UK job market, you are at a big disadvantage.

The solution: Get locally qualified in a skilled area!

Get an NVQ or professional qualification where you have to become a member of a professional body. A good example is AAT/CIMA/ACA/ACCA/CIPFA in Accountancy. Choose jobs with maths, science, or economics components. Brits are not fond of these subjects. Start at the bottom and work your way up. Don't expect to start at a high level.

National Vocational Qualifications (NVQs) are work based awards in England, Wales and Northern Ireland that are achieved through assessment and training.

The best employer in Britain

Public sector jobs offer good pay, job-security, pension and best of all: no discrimination against foreigners.

Public sector workers earn up to £3,200 a year more than their private sector equivalents in similar professions. In some parts of the North East, Merseyside and the South West, public sector workers are paid as much as 14 per cent more – or £3,200 a year on average.

A report revealed in 2014 that even after a three-year pay squeeze public sector workers continue to enjoy an average 'pay premium' of more than six per cent over private sector workers.

However, in central London, the East and South East, the average public sector worker is paid less than they would if they were working in the private sector (source: think-tank Policy Exchange).

More than 12 per cent of UK GDP – £180 billion – is spent on public sector pay. On average, a public sector worker benefits from a 6.1 per cent pay premium, earning as much as £1,400 a year more than someone in the private sector. Women tend to have larger pay premiums than men.

Jobs or careers that foreigners usually take in Britain

Any jobs that the local people cannot take easily, or will not take easily are taken by foreigners. Jobs like these given below tend to be chosen by foreigners:

- Lawyer/Solicitor
- IT Professional
- Accountant
- Doctor of Medicine/GP
- Nurse
- Economist
- Statistician
- Pharmacist
- Optometrist
- Bus/Taxi Driver
- Carer
- Cleaner

Jobs requiring arduous study/odd hours of work/ or jobs that are themselves arduous or viewed as boring tend to be avoided by locals. Foreigners who don't get jobs, because of poor English or no qualifications, tend to run restaurants, corner shops, newsagents, pharmacies, taxis and post offices (all favourites of Asians) or non-supermarket petrol stations (dominated by Sri Lankan Tamils). Fruit/vegetable picking and packing are also jobs often taken by foreigners with poor English.

Jobs facing staff shortages

The UK is suffering one of the worst skills shortages in Europe, according to a study by recruitment firm Hays. Its annual Global Skills Index indicates that the UK's economic recovery is exposing skills shortages across multiple industries.

Job opportunities in industries such as oil and gas, energy, IT and construction have grown over the past year but the necessary skilled employees are not available locally according to Hays.

Doctors, Midwives, Engineers, Head Teachers, Maths and Science Teachers, Accountants, People with foreign language skills and Social Workers are some professions facing staff shortages in the UK. The author has written a book on this subject *Best UK Jobs For Foreigners: Jobs with less competition from Britons* (available on Amazon). This book is given to you free within this book.

Chapter 5. Beat the High Cost of UK Public Transport

Pressure on roads and public transport

Britain has an expensive public transport system. Even if public transport were free and reliable, people would still prefer cars. Learn to drive asap (as soon as possible) and you can be more flexible in your life about where you live, work or study.

Drivers, however, must be prepared for other problems. Commuting is a nightmare in many places. This means stressful early mornings, delays on roads, and long journeys commuting. It gets worse in winter when one has to contend with frost on the car, ice on the roads, and poor visibility due to fog. Those living in London or near it may have no option but to commute using public transport because parking may be unavailable or too expensive there. Parking in London costs an average of £42 per day.

Those driving in to central London have to pay the £10 congestion charge as well. You have to pay a £10 daily charge if you drive between 07:00 and 18:00, Monday to Friday in the Congestion Charge Zone. There is no charge on weekends, public holidays, between Christmas Day and New Year's Day inclusive, or between 18:00 and 07:00 on weekdays.

Commuters to London generally use public transport for commuting to London (train+London Underground or train+bus).

Ways you can save money on train ticket prices

According to a report by the trade union TUC an average commute in the UK is 67 minutes long. A journey lasting 1 hour into central London can cost between £7000-10,000 per year on a monthly season ticket. You can include the payment for the London underground when you buy your train ticket. If you are a commuter, you have to factor the travel costs into your decision to work in London. A weekly ticket often costs less than two dailies.

• Book well in advance (you can book upto 3 months in advance). Check out www.redspottedhanky.com for good deals on train tickets bought in advance. Buying on the day is costliest.

• Look for last minute deals before you travel. Sign up with Amazon Local for such deals.

• Get yourself a Railcard (£30/year) and save a third off fares.

• Buy a season ticket and get a bulk-buy discount. Sometimes breaking a long journey into two season tickets or two or more tickets can save you money.

• Sometimes two single fares can be cheaper than a return.

• Remember that peak time fares (travelling before 10 am and between 4-7pm) are higher.

Carry a bicycle on trains: You are allowed to carry bicycles on British trains. You can cycle part of the journey and save money on the London Tube, buses or taxis. Some people even carry folding bicycles on the train. You can buy a folding bicycle for between £140-200.

Chapter 6. Warnings on the Effects of Population Growth

Rising population growth and density

Figures from Eurostat reveal that the UK is the most densely populated country in Europe. It also has Europe's highest population growth rate. About a third of this growth came from immigration. The UK also has the second-highest birth rate in Europe. The number of live births in Britain was 813,000 in 2012, compared to France (822,000) which was first.

England (at 395 people per square kilometre) is the third most densely populated major country in the world after Bangladesh (1045) and South Korea (498). Within Europe, England already has the highest population density (Malta is higher, but it is a very small country). England's population density has risen from 244 in 2006 and is presently double that of Germany and four times that of France.

This means that there is considerable demand for space in the UK. Space is a luxury in this country. Be warned: this means that even if you can afford a house in this country it is not likely to be a large one, unless you are extremely wealthy. Rents are likely to be very high in and around London.

Apart from housing, the high population growth also means great pressure on jobs, roads, school places, and hospital services.

Pressure on school places

The chances of your child studying in a crowded classroom are increasing day by day. There are already 77 primary schools in England with more than 800 pupils. The government provided an extra 90,000 primary school places in England in 2013, but that was not found to be enough. An additional 130,000 places will be needed by 2017 according to the Local Government Association (LGA).

Almost half of England's school districts will have more primary school pupils than places by 2015.

Some local areas will face a 20% shortfall in places by 2015, according to analysis of official data from 2012.

What is causing this pressure on school places?

The answer: rising birth rate and immigration. According to the Office for National Statistics, more babies were born in the UK in 2011-12 than any year since 1972. In the same year, 165,600 more people came to the UK than left - contributing to an overall rise in UK population of 419,900.

The LGA's analysis of local authority data on school-place needs suggests about 1,000 of the 2,277 local school planning districts will be over-capacity by 2015-16. The greatest pressure is focused on about 99 districts, where 20% more pupils are predicted than places.

Overall, two thirds of local authorities are predicting they will have more pupils than places by the beginning of the 2016 academic year. Some 40 local councils are predicted to be 10% over capacity, with 15 of those predicting a 20% surplus of pupils over places.

High property prices

High property prices are another potential problem. New migrants will have a hard time buying a house in Britain unless they are very high earners or are living far away from property hotspots. Where there are plenty of jobs (London and the South East) there is far too much demand for housing and not enough housing available. New migrants may be forced to migrate to cheaper places in the UK, but may have to contend with a job shortage there. Even if house prices fall there may be difficulty getting a mortgage, unless they are permanent residents, have a high income and a huge deposit (at least 25% of the house price).

To add to their property woes, people in Britain pay higher property taxes than any other country in the 33 member Organisation for Economic Co-operation and Development (OECD). Property taxes paid in the UK amount to £60billion a year. Charges like stamp duty, council tax, capital gains tax, inheritance tax and business rates are higher in the UK than any of the other members of the OECD.

The average size of a new build home in the UK is quite small: 76 sq.m. New build homes in some European countries are bigger: Ireland 87.7 sq.m; Netherlands 115.5 sq.m; Denmark 137 sq.m. Source: Royal Institute of British Architects.

According to research conducted by property website zoopla.co.uk for The Telegraph, the total number of homes valued at more than £1million grew to a total of 427,501 in April 2014.

More than half of these, 271,000, were in London, where average prices have risen to £414,490. The average cost of a three-bed family home in 'prime' areas of London is now £1.67million and expected to rise to £2million by 2015.

Pressure on the NHS

In many parts of the UK health care services are under great stress due to many reasons:

- An ageing population,
- Shortage of doctors,
- Shortage of dentists,
- Shortage of nurses and midwives,

- High cost of providing free health care to all

- and influx of new migrants to the UK.

It is very hard to get a doctor's appointment instantly by calling on the same day. You may have high fever today but the quickest appointment you can get may be one week later. In winter, this could be three weeks later. Faced with this situation most people go to A&E (Accident and Emergency).

Maternity services have been hard hit due to the shortage of midwives - see chapter on immigration for more. The UK is also facing a severe shortage of qualified dentists. You must count yourself lucky if you can register with an NHS dentist in the UK and receive reasonably priced (not free) dental care. Dentists have been leaving the NHS in droves and joining private practice because the latter is more lucrative.

The NHS is running out of money and struggles to meet the needs of the soaring population, the elderly and the obese, according to Dr Mark Porter, the chairman of the British Medical Association's council. He said the financial outlook was dire and the health service was 'struggling just to keep pace' with rising demand. And he said that within the next ten years, if funding only keeps pace with inflation, the NHS could have annual debts of up to £54billion as patient demand far outstrips the money it gets from the Treasury.

The health service has an annual budget of £106 billion and unlike other Government departments it has been protected from public service cuts over the past three years.

But there is mounting concern among doctors and healthcare leaders that even if this level of income is guaranteed, the service will not be able to meet the soaring demand. This is because of the rising population, increased numbers of elderly, the effects of obesity and alcohol and the cost of expensive new medicines.

Chapter 7. Living and Working Efficiently

Where to live and work

High property prices in London are a potential problem in the UK. New migrants will have a hard time buying a house in London unless they are very high earners. Where there are plenty of jobs (London and the South East) there is far too much demand for housing and not enough housing stock available.

But London has the jobs people need, and salaries are higher because of London weighting – a system of higher pay for London's workers. The solution favoured by many is this: work in London but live outside London.

Every day, armies of people travel into London from nearby towns and cities by road, and train. Early morning trains to London are packed with commuters heading to work. Government statistics estimate that at peak times about 20% of travelers to London travel standing. Train services into London Paddington are said to be the most crowded.

Most trains have Wi-Fi so travelers can be online on their smartphone, tablet or laptop. Train ticket prices are designed in such a manner that it is far cheaper to buy a weekly ticket than two daily tickets. Working in London does not favour those who work one or two days a week there.

The top 20 commuter hotspots around London

According to a report by estate agents Savills (published in the Daily Telegraph), the top 20 commuter hotspots around London are:

Commuter hotspot, Proportion of commuters to London (%), Average house price there

1. Brentwood, Essex, 24.4, £341,059

2. Elmbrigde, Surrey, 21.5, £591,361

3. Epsom and Ewell, Surrey, 21.4, £351,068

4. Sevenoaks, Kent, 20.3, £391,327

5. St.Albans, Hertfordshire, 19.3, £419,697

6. Tandridge, Surrey, 18.4, £355,141

7. Dartford, Kent, 17.7, £213,959

8. Epping Forest, Essex, 17.5, £349,726

9. Basildon, Essex, 17.0, £216,720

10. Thurrock, Essex, 16.7, £180,479

11. Woking, Surrey, 16.2, £345,691

12. Rochford, Essex, 16.0, £235,912

13. Southend-on-sea, Essex,16.0, £211,465

14. Hertsmere, Hertfordshire, 15.5, £376,312

15. Reigate and Banstead, Surrey, 15.4, £334,847

16. Tunbridge Wells, Kent, 14.9, £325,764

17. Castle Point, Essex, 14.1, £211,441

18. Watford, Hertfordshire, 14.1, £261,807

19. East Hertfordshire, 13.9, £311,550

20. Broxbourne, Hertfordshire, 13.9, £245,585

New migrants may be forced to migrate to cheaper places in the UK, but there may have to contend with a job shortage. Even if house prices fall, as they did slightly between 2008-2012, there may be difficulty getting a mortgage, unless they are permanent residents, have a high income and a huge deposit (at least 25% of the house price).

Chapter 8. Advice for Your Family

Don't Lose Your Kids

An epidemic of family breakup is sweeping Britain. According to a report by the Marriage Foundation think tank, children born in 2012 are more likely than any previous generation to see their parents split up. Nearly half will experience family breakdown. The foundation estimates that 354,000 out of the 729,674 children born in England and Wales in 2012 will have parents who are separated by the time they reach the age of 15. It concludes that it is the declining rates of marriage which provide the explanation for the doubling of family breakdown since the 1980s.

There were 241,100 weddings in England and Wales in 2010 compared with more than 400,000 a year in the early 1970s. In 2009, there were only 232,443 weddings – the lowest number since the 19th century.

Around five million parents have gone through separation and the figures from the Dept. of Work and Pensions show over four million children in 2012 lived in separated families - equal to 30% of children in Britain. According to the Office for National Statistics, the number of over-60s in England and Wales getting divorced is also rising.

In 1991, there were 1.6 divorces per 1,000 married men over 60, but by 2011, the latest year for which figures are available, this had risen to 2.3.

There were 1.2 divorces per 1,000 married women over 60 in 1991, rising to 1.6 in 2011.

Reasons for this increase include the pressures facing couples as they grow older, changes arising from children leaving home or going to university, and the wish to pursue other relationships later on in life.

The 2011 Census showed a 20% increase in the number of people in England and Wales whose marriages had collapsed, compared with a decade before.

There are now more than four million divorcees and more than a million people who are separated.

Findings from the Centre for Social Justice have shown as many as one million children are growing up without a father.

The Centre has also linked family breakdown to the likelihood of children being involved in truancy, juvenile delinquency and alcohol or drug abuse.

Family breakup can cause parents to lose their kids.

The UK is facing a decline of the family as a social unit. Children are keen to go their own way, and do their own thing (smoke, drink alcohol, sleep with their boyfriend/girlfriend etc... all in their teens) regardless of whether their parents think it wise or not. A new migrant's children could be heading this way unless they take steps to keep the family together.

The best free schools in the UK

A grammar school is a state school for the academically gifted. Admissions are by entrance test only, not by catchment area. It is a system by which pupils can get a good education by merit rather than through family income. Pupils who study in top grammar schools find getting admission into the best universities much easier.

Universities tend to be influenced by the secondary school where your child studied in deciding admission. Foreigners rush to these schools because they offer an excellent opportunity for the children of the middle classes to get into top jobs and become part of the elite of this country. If your child is bright and can pass the entrance test of your local grammar school, you are strongly advised to choose the grammar school option. You can then get a top quality education for your child without paying any fees.

Getting into the catchment area

A catchment area refers to the particular streets that a school serves. Families living on those streets have first priority in admissions to that school. If a school is good the demand by parents to live in the catchment area pushes up house prices on those streets. If you like a particular school move into its catchment area. If you can't afford to buy a property there then rent a property in that catchment area and live there. This is acceptable for school admissions. Some local councils may have rules requiring you to actually live there for a while and require you to produce proof of residence (usually utility bills).

Many unscrupulous parents rent an additional property merely to get into a school. This is an unfair practice. They do this because in many London boroughs there are no rules against it. The attraction to do this is also because once a child gets into a particular school their sibling can also get in, even if the family no longer live near that school.

Beware of allergies

One in three Britons suffers from an allergy. It could be allergies to nuts, dust mites, pollen, milk, pets, mould or many others. The fact that British children spend less time outdoors and consequently are exposed to less bacteria has been found to be one of the main reasons. Other reasons attributed include the use of antibiotics in early age, the rise in caesarean births, and not being breast-fed in childhood. The British trend towards keeping squeaky-clean homes may also play its part.

Chapter 9. Settling Down in Britain Permanently

Settling down in Britain is one of the most important questions that concern foreigners. On the question of settling down in Britain permanently there are four main routes:

• Marrying a local, or a person having permanent residency, and then applying to settle down permanently (but beware of doing a sham marriage!).

• Living here legally for 10 years and then applying to settle down permanently.

• Living here illegally for 20 years and then applying to settle down permanently (not recommended).

• Working here legally for five years and then applying to settle down permanently. (Check latest Home Office rules on this here: http://www.ukba.homeoffice.gov.uk/visas-immigration/settlement/).

There are other ways in which this can be done, but note that there are no published rules about these, only conventions. One convention that has consistently worked for many people is explained below.

The UK authorities tend to grant permanent residency to applicants who can prove that they have lived in the UK legally for seven years and throughout this period a child of theirs has lived with them. It is essential that the child has not been away from the UK for more than two months at a time during this period and any absences have been infrequent and finally the applicant must prove that they have lost ties with their home country. This is done to protect the child's human rights because it would be unfair to send back a child who has become accustomed to living in the UK after over seven years of continuous legal residency.

Want to know more about UK Immigration? The author has written a book exclusively on this subject. It is called **UK Immigration Made Simple: Taking the Complexity out of UK Immigration Rules.** It is available on all Amazon websites in digital and paperback formats.

Chapter 10. Securing Funding for Studying in the UK

There are more than 3,000 different scholarships available for study in the UK. The number of scholarships available are too numerous to list for students from all countries. A few important ones for non-EU overseas students are listed in the next section below.

The first step is to contact the British Council in your country for advice. They usually have a Scholarships Officer for help and advice. Alternately, read the Prospectus of the university of your choice either in a British Council library near you or online and find out. All scholarships offered by a university are listed on its prospectus.

It is important to visit the website of Education UK (a branch of the British Council) at http://www.educationuk.org/Scholarships-for-UK-study for more information. Here you can search for scholarships available by putting in your study details.

There are other good ways of funding your studies after you join the university even if you don't get a full scholarship. After you arrive, apply to your university for scholarships for international students. Universities usually have scholarships for international students of good academic ability that takes 25% off your tuition fees. Secondly, a Research Studentship may be available for postgraduate study. Speak to your Head of Department. Look for short-term Research Assistantships if you are a postgraduate student. These are advertised in the departmental notice boards. Postgraduate students are also called upon to do tutorials for undergraduate students for which the university usually will pay well. If all else fails, try the university's Hardship Fund for help. Students are also known to take up part-time work (in supermarkets) in order to pay for their studies.

Some major scholarships available to non-EU students are given below:

Commonwealth Scholarships and Fellowships plan

Cambridge Fellowships

British Chevening Scholarships

Felix Scholarship (available only at Reading University, Oxford University, and SOAS London). This scholarship pays fees, living costs, travel expenses, money for books and warm clothes.

Royal Society Fellowships (only available for Postdoctoral studies).

Saltire Scholarships (for study in Scotland. Upto 200 awards worth £2000 each. These are towards the tuition fees, for any one year of full time study, on an Undergraduate, Masters or PhD course at any of Scotland's higher education institutions. Available to students from China, Canada, India and the USA).

Dorothy Hodgkin Postgraduate Awards (DHPA) is a UK scheme to bring outstanding students from India, China, Hong Kong, South Africa, Brazil, Russia and the developing world to come and study for PhDs in top UK research facilities. Each scholarship is jointly funded by one public sector (Research Council) and one private sector partner. The scheme is open to top quality science, engineering, medicine, social science and technology students from overseas to study for PhDs over a period of three to four years, at an average annual cost per student of £30,000 (each DHPA is valued at £90,000) primarily to cover fees and maintenance. Contact the university where you are planning to study for more information, for e.g. see this webpage Cardiff University).

Inlaks scholarships (only available to students from India).

Also see these websites for more information:

British Council (http://www.educationuk.org/global/)

Economic and Social Research Council (http://www.esrc.ac.uk/funding-and-guidance/funding-opportunities/).

Those interested in finding out more on studying in the UK can refer to the author's books

Study in the UK: All Your Questions Answered or

Best Scholarships for Studying in the UK: Study in the UK for Free!

(a very big list of scholarships for UK studies are listed in these books)

Best UK Jobs for Foreigners

Britain has an ageing society. About 20% of the population are pensioners. An ageing society has problems paying it's pensions because there are less people of working age around. To compound matters, there are less skilled people of working age around than needed. What can the government do?

One solution is to raise the retirement age for pension, making people work longer. The government has done that. Immigration of young, skilled and hardworking people is the other solution.

Britain's Office of Budget Responsibility has found that allowing more than 140,000 immigrants into Britain a year, equivalent to about 7 million people in 50 years, would help increase the overall number of people who are in work and improve public finances.

What are the areas in which skills shortages exist in the UK?

Which skilled jobs are desperately in need of foreigners because of the local unavailability of talent?

In which skilled profession is talent in such short supply that temporary staff can earn as much as £15,000 per week?

Do UK employers like the work ethic of foreigners?

Are those with foreign language skills in demand?

What is the government's official view on the UK's skills shortages?

Find answers to these and other similar questions in this book.

This book below is one of Rajiv Immanuel's series of books designed to help foreigners considering the UK as a place to live, work or study. As a first step, anyone considering coming to live in these shores needs to know what employment they could possibly take up, where there would be less competition from locals.

The book mentioned below does just that:

Best UK Jobs for Foreigners

This book is given to you free below.

Britain – A Land of Opportunity

The UK Skills Crisis

There are plenty of vacancies in the UK but about 20% cannot be filled because there are not enough skilled people available in the country. What are those areas? That is the subject matter of this part of the book.

The UKCES (the UK Commission for Employment and Skills) in a survey of 91,000 employers found more than 20% of vacancies in the UK were down to a poor skills base. It found 146,200 job vacancies (22%) in 2013 were unfilled because of inadequate skills, compared with 91,400 (16%) in 2011.

As at January 2014, about 22% or 124,800 of 559,600 job vacancies in England are so-called "skills shortage vacancies." There are skills gaps in science, technology, engineering and maths in the UK.

Immigration is the solution at the moment. According to Britain's Office of National Statistics (ONS), the number of foreign workers taking jobs in the UK has increased by 225,000 to 4.26 million in a year, compared with a rise of 192,000 for British-born workers.

The UKCES says employers in the UK are struggling to find employees with the "core generic skills" of communication, literacy and numeracy. One of the main reasons for this situation is not only a lack of skilled young people but also a lack of young people in general due to the ageing population.

The UK's Ageing Population

In Western societies, higher quality health care, better nutrition, access to clean water and in general better government has had one major effect: people live longer.

Spain, Italy, France and Japan are the toppers when it comes to the numbers of those over 100 years of age.

In Japan, for instance, there were (in 2012) 1,1197 people aged 90 or over per 100,000 people. In contrast, in India there were only 58 people aged 90 or over per 100,000 people.

The UK is next highest. The UK is not too far behind Japan. There were 823 people aged 90 or over per 100,000 people in the UK.

In 1982 there were 2560 people in the UK over the age of 100. In 2012, there were 12,320 according to the Office for National Statistics (ONS) – a five-fold increase. More than 600 of these were aged over 105.

The population of the over-90s - a group the ONS calls the "very old" - increased by 33% from 2002 to 2012. There are about half a million people in this category.

In 2012, there were 13,350 people over 100 years old living in Britain, from 7,740 in 2002: an increase of 73%.

10 million people in the UK are over 65 years old.

The latest (2013) government projections are for 5½ million more elderly people in 20 years time and the number will have nearly doubled to around 19 million by 2050.

In 2008 there were 3.2 people of working age for every person of pensionable age. This ratio is projected to fall to 2.8 by 2033. People are living longer. A man born in the UK in 1981 had a life expectancy at birth of 84 years. For a boy born in 2013, that figure is 89 years, and by 2030 it is projected to be 91. The trend for women is similar.

There are also one million more pensioners than there were a decade ago and 600,000 more full time unpaid carers, while one in six Britons is over 65.

Britain has an ageing population. Britons are living longer. This means that they will need to have their state pensions paid for by others for longer. The post war baby boom has added more people for whom pensions have to be paid. Who pays for these pensions?

The UK Pensions Crisis

The state pension is paid for by current taxpayers. If there were plenty of young people to work and pay the pensions for the elderly there would be no pension issue. But there is a shortage of young, hard working, skilled people in the UK workforce. So who will pay the pensions of the future?

One way out is for people to work longer after retirement. This has been allowed by the government. The age of retirement is called the State Pension Age (SPA). Currently it is 65 for men and 60 for women. The state pension age is planned to be equalised for men and women at age 65, and is then going to rise to 66 for both men and women by 2020, and then to 67 by 2028. People are making use of this facility to work longer.

Figures available with the Office for National Statistics suggest that the number of people in the UK working beyond the state pension age has almost doubled since 1993, to stand at 1.41 million in 2011. This reflects not only a growing and ageing population, but pressure to keep on earning beyond retirement age. About two thirds of those working beyond SPA are working part-time. And just over half work for small employers, who are more likely not to provide a pension scheme. There may be many factors influencing the decision for more people to work past SPA such as the improved health and well-being of this group, financial pressures, people living longer and wanting to remain active in society and others. About half of UK workers do not have or save into a pension scheme. Working past retirement age to make ends meet is one way out.

The other solution to meet pension payments is to permit the immigration of young, skilled workers into the country, which is being done by the government, albeit with less fanfare. This thinking was probably behind the UK Labour government's allowing of record levels of immigration into the country during its term in office (1997-2010).

More foreigners came to Britain during 2001-2011 (2.9 million) than in the previous 50 years (2.7 million).

The effects of an ageing society

This ageing of the UK's population has considerable consequences for public services. Britain's Office for Budget Responsibility (OBR) has said that spending on the state pension, social care and healthcare (National Health Service) will rise from 14% of Britain's GDP to almost 20%.

The OECD (Organisation for Economic Cooperation and Development) warned (in 2013) that unless action was taken to cut the cost to the state of Britain's rapidly rising elderly population, the UK's health and pensions systems could collapse.

The OBR report found that allowing more than 140,000 immigrants into Britain a year, equivalent to about 7 million people in 50 years, would help increase the overall number of people who are in work and improve public finances. Without action to address the burden of an ageing population, the UK will be left with a £65 billion deficit in its public finances, according to the OBR report

The conclusion is clear. The UK has a shortage of labour particularly skilled labour (those with high quality vocational and technical skills). It has an ageing population: 20% of the population are pensioners. The over-85s are the fastest growing section of the population. This means the UK will always need young skilled workers. The average age of the population is 39 and the average number of children per family has dropped from 2.0 in 1971 to 1.8 in 2013. This accounts for the shortage of labour in the economy. The only way forward to meet state-pension payments for the future is to increase the retirement age and/or to take in more foreign workers. These facts show that there are many opportunities for skilled, hard-working and young immigrants.

Britain needs millions more immigrants over the next 50 years to reduce the "unsustainable" pressure that the ageing population is putting on the economy.

Pressure on the NHS

In many parts of the UK health care services are under great stress due to many reasons:

- An ageing population,

- Shortage of doctors,

- Shortage of dentists,

- Shortage of nurses and midwives,

- High cost of providing free health care to all

- influx of new migrants to the UK

- Rising birth rate

It is very hard to get a doctor's appointment instantly by calling on the same day. You may have high fever today but the quickest appointment you can get may be one week later. In winter this could be three weeks later. Faced with this situation most people go to A&E (Accident and Emergency).

Maternity services have been hard hit due to the shortage of midwives - see chapter on immigration for more. The UK is also facing a severe shortage of qualified dentists. You must count yourself lucky if you can register with an NHS dentist in the UK and receive reasonably priced (not free) dental care. Dentists have been leaving the NHS in droves and joining private practice because the latter is more lucrative.

The NHS is running out of money and struggles to meet the needs of the soaring population, the elderly and the obese, according to Dr Mark Porter, the chairman of the British Medical Association's council. He said the financial outlook was dire and the health service was 'struggling just to keep pace' with rising demand. And he said that within the next ten years, if funding only keeps pace with inflation, the NHS could have annual debts of up to £54billion as patient demand far outstrips the money it gets from the Treasury.

The health service has an annual budget of £106 billion and unlike other Government departments it has been protected from public service cuts over the past three years. But there is mounting concern among doctors and healthcare leaders that even if this level of income is guaranteed, the service will not be able to meet the soaring demand. This is because of the rising population, increased numbers of elderly, the effects of obesity and alcohol and the cost of expensive new medicines.

The UK Needs foreign doctors

The doctor shortage

Britain has fewer doctors per person than nearly all other European countries, according to a report by the European Commission. The report ranks the UK 24th out of 27 countries in the EU, ahead of only Poland, Romania and Slovenia. There are an average of 2.71 medics for every 1,000 people, compared to six in Greece, five in Austria and nearly four in Italy.

The UK National Health Service (NHS) desperately needs foreign doctors. According to Clare Gerada, chair of the Royal College of GPs, Britain's surgeries are short of GPs (General Practitioner) and the doctor shortage number has been estimated as 10,000. There is also a shortage of doctors in the UK willing to work evenings and weekends.

Rajiv Immanuel

Hiring temporary doctors

Hospitals and doctors' surgeries have to provide medical staff as temporary cover to maintain health care services where there are staff shortages. To cope with these shortages a lucrative market for temporary doctors in the UK has opened up.

News reports indicate that the NHS has been hiring locum (temporary) doctors from Lithuania, Poland, Germany, Hungary, Italy and Switzerland because of this shortage. The NHS relies on foreign doctors because a 2003 contract for British GPs has resulted in more than 90 per cent opting out of responsibility for their patients in the evenings and at weekends. As a result of the agreement, most surgeries now subcontract out-of-hours work to private firms.

Added to this, a government decision to sign up to the European Working Time Directive, which set a maximum 48-hour-week for doctors in August 2009, has meant that many hospitals have had to either take on more doctors, or use staff from agencies, which recruit from elsewhere in the UK and abroad.

From data obtained by Labour under the Freedom of Information Act it is clear that NHS spending on locum doctors to plug the gaps in A&E units in England has risen by 60% in three years. £83.3m was spent in 2013, up from £52m in 2009-10.

There are about 15,000 locum doctors working in the UK. Many newly qualified UK doctors also work as locums to gain experience. Many overseas doctors find working as locums useful as a way of getting into the system.

Highly qualified temporary doctors can be paid as much as £15,000 per week. Less highly qualified doctors earn about £100-200 per hour or about £1500 per shift.

According to industry sources, general practice locums earn more than hospital locums. This is because the latter have income tax and national insurance deducted before they are paid, and there is less scope for legitimate tax deductions for expenses like maintaining a car, telephone charges, printing, stationery, and accountancy fees.

It is relatively easy to find work through an agency and the locum doctor will be paid at a significantly higher hourly rate than the incumbent doctor will.

The potential for locum work in general practice is enormous and so is attractive to different groups of doctors.

Locum work is flexible and interesting. It gives the doctor the chance to see many aspects of medicine without the requirement of a long term commitment early in a career. With the ever increasing demands for a better quality of life, part time work in an unstructured or semi structured form is possible. Locums are recruited for a variety of reasons, including the creation of new posts, when a post cannot be filled, and to cover sickness and maternity leave.

Are you a doctor willing to go and work in places where UK doctors are less willing to go?

· A North Wales hospital trust spent £50 million on locum doctors between the years 2010 – 2013.

· Many hospitals in Scotland are unable to attract doctors to permanent positions particularly at the level of consultants. A hospital trust in Scotland (Dumfries and Galloway) had 12 vacancies of consultants in 2013. According to its medical director the service is maintained by locum doctors.

Heavy pressure on A&E

According to an estimate by the Royal College of General Practitioners about 26.2 million patients in the UK wait a week before they are able to see a GP and about 46.8 million wait a week before they can speak to a nurse at their practice. These effects are because of a rising population and shortage of GPs. The result is tremendous pressure on A&E (Accident and Emergency).

The shortage of GPs has caused a crisis in UK A&E departments, with high numbers of patients turning up at A&E because their usual surgeries are closed on evenings and weekends. Over the past decade the number of patients turning up in A&E has risen by a third. According to the National Audit Office there were 21.7million such attendances in 2012. The staggering rise has partly been blamed on a failure of GP out-of-hours services, which has left patients with nowhere else to go, as well as a rise in the elderly population.

In Devon and Cornwall there is a shortage of A&E doctors. Dr Clifford Mann, of the College of Emergency Medicine (CEM), said in 2013 that less than 50% of training places had been taken up in two years. Dr Mann, who is based at Musgrove Park Hospital in Somerset, said: "For two years running we've had only 50% people that we expected to be training in emergency medicine." He said gaps in rotas were being filled by staff working overtime, or by drafting in locums who were expensive to employ.

According to UK Health minister Dr Dan Poulter: "Recruiting and holding on to doctors in A&E has been a problem for over a decade - A&E is not a popular choice among trainees and in recent years less than 50% of the speciality training places available were taken."

Recruitment of A&E doctors is an ongoing problem, and the crisis is worsening. Half the vacancies across the country are going unfilled, stretching staff further and further. Retaining A&E doctors is also a problem in the NHS.

The reason why recruitment of doctors to A&E departments is a problem is because it is seen as a dirty job with unsociable hours. It is also not as well paid as other medical specialities because there is no scope for private work.

To cope with the staffing crisis many recruitment firms are offering hospitals doctors who normally work as GPs to work in A&E at weekends. They are known to be offering them payments of around £1500 per shift of 12 hours in London.

What are the effects of the doctor shortage?

Dr Chaand Nagpaul, the GPs Committee Chairman at the British Medical Association has warned: "General practice is under real pressure from spiralling patient demand, especially from an ageing population, and falling resources."

More than 3,500 people died unnecessarily in NHS hospitals in 2012-13 because of mistakes and blunders. The number of 'avoidable' deaths admitted by NHS trusts in England rose by 25 per cent in a year, while experts warned overcrowding could contribute to even more fatalities in overstretched hospitals in winter. The figures include cases where patients have died after being given the wrong medicines, have suffered fatal surgical mistakes or simply died because staff failed to spot they were deteriorating fast.

The new figures, from the National Reporting and Learning System, show the number of patients who died due to safety incidents rose from 2,864 in 2011/12 to 3,588 in 2012/13.

The UK desperately needs locum GPs and hospital locum doctors. The UK Home Office indicates that the following medical jobs are in the shortage list:

Jobs on the UK Shortage Occupation List

· trainees in paediatrics or anaesthetics

· staff doctors in paediatrics or anaesthetics

· consultants in paediatrics or anaesthetics

· non-consultant, non-training doctors in the specialty obstetrics and gynaecology

Salary details:

Speciality registrar and equivalent: £29,705

Speciality doctor and equivalent: £36,807

Salaried General practitioner (GP) and equivalent: £53,781

Consultant and equivalent: £74,504

(source: UK Home Office)

The UK Needs midwives

The UK has had a higher teenage pregnancy rate compared to West European countries for many years. In 2010, the teenage pregnancy rate fell for the first time since 1969 according to figures from the Office for National Statistics. This has been attributed to the dedicated work of professionals in relationship and sex education, contraception and local services. In 2010, 6674 girls under 16 and 34,633 under 18s became pregnant in England and Wales.

In 2013, more than 48,000 babies were born to teenage mothers in Britain. British rates of teenage pregnancy remain far behind those of the USA however. In the USA, 1 in 20 girls has babies each year compared to 1 in 34 in the UK.

Britain's high teenage pregnancy rate is not because of ignorance of contraceptive use. A report by Prince Charles's charity the Prince's Trust said teenage single girls on council estates admire their peers who have given birth and often seek to copy their status and acquire a council flat. Britain's teenage mums cost the taxpayer an estimated £125million in income support alone every year and Housing Benefit.

Among older women, the pregnancy rate overall has increased, as more women in their 30s and 40s are now having babies. The sharpest rise occurred among women aged 40 and over, rising by 5.2% to nearly 30,000. The over-40 pregnancy rate has more than doubled since 1990. The Royal College of Midwives has said it was concerned that pregnancy rates overall are still rising and that midwife numbers have not kept pace.

Studying to be a midwife would appear to be a wise career choice.

The UK Needs Nurses

According to the Royal College of Nursing (RCN) the UK is heading for a nursing shortage that could have serious implications for health services and patients. Since 2010, there have been cuts to student nursing places and nursing posts. Nurses are under increased pressure to see more patients and the ones with greater needs, because there are fewer staff to look after them.

A newly qualified nurse in the NHS earns £21,176 a year. In 2013, there were about 87,000 foreign nurses in the UK. Most of them came from Australia, Philippines, South Africa, India, and Zimbabwe. According to the Nursing and Midwifery Council (NWC) over 16,000 of the 670,000 nurses in the UK were from the Philippines alone. There are also a number of nurses in the UK from within the EU. Over 3000 nurses from European countries registered with the NWC in 2012.

According to Nursingtimes.net, which produces the UK's weekly nursing magazine, the annual Royal College of Nursing Labour Market review, a combination of the squeeze on NHS finances, reductions in places on nursing courses, and a higher number of nurses moving abroad than are coming to the UK, means a nursing shortage is looming.

At least 40 hospital trusts have actively recruited nurses from abroad, with 1,360 nurses being signed up from countries from Spain and Portugal to Australia and the Philippines. With another 41 planning to launch recruitment drives, and NHS recruitment fairs scheduled for Madrid and Lisbon in 2014, the number is expected to rise.

Are you going to be around and ready when the government starts recruiting nurses again?

The UK Needs Accountants

Being an Accountant is one of the best jobs for foreigners in the UK. There is a shortage of CCAB qualified Accountants in the areas in and around London. CCAB refers to the Consultative Committee of Accountancy Bodies (CCAB), an umbrella group of chartered professional bodies of British qualified accountants. As of 2013, CCAB had five member bodies:

- Association of Chartered Certified Accountants (ACCA)

- Chartered Institute of Public Finance and Accountancy (CIPFA)

- Institute of Chartered Accountants in England and Wales (ICAEW)

- Institute of Chartered Accountants of Scotland (ICAS)

The sixth founder member was the Chartered Institute of Management Accountants (CIMA).

When job advertisements mention "CCAB qualified" they generally mean CIMA as well, even though CIMA left the CCAB in 2011.

Local government councils in and around London struggle to recruit and crucially retain professionally qualified accountants. The shortage of CCAB qualified accountants has made many accountants turn 'Consultant' instead.

A typical consultant's money-making strategy goes like this. They avoid regular employment in a Local Government Council at about £45,000- 50,000 per year (Senior Finance Manager). They instead work for daily wages (usually about £400-500 per day). The Consultants earn £150,000 per year instead. They work through agencies who keep them regularly employed. Some of them work for only a few months with any particular government body and then move on to the next contract.

Every day, websites such as http://www.jobsgopublic.com/ (dedicated to public sector jobs) carry many advertisements for qualified accountants. Do check this out if you are a CCAB qualified accountant looking for a job in and around London.

If you are not an accountant, and would like to study to be one, try to acquire a CCAB qualification. Visit the websites mentioned above and choose the accountancy qualification that suits your interests. Note that the CIPFA accountancy qualification is specific to public sector. Public sector is one of the best employers for foreigners because they follow the government's equal opportunities policy.

Shortage of Maths and Science Graduates in the UK

The UK government's Plan for Growth attaches great importance to education and the hi-tech industry to create jobs and prosperity. But there is a shortage of science graduates in the UK with maths skills. Not only is there a shortage of science graduates with maths skills, the quality of maths skills they possess is not up to the mark. This is the conclusion of the UK House of Lords Science and Technology Committee.

England is the only developed country producing children who are worse at reading and maths than their grandparents, according to a recent report from the Organisation for Economic Co-operation and Development. In the OECD's shocking assessment of October 2013: "England is the only country where the oldest age group has higher proficiency in both literacy and numeracy than the youngest group, after other factors, such as gender, socio-economic backgrounds and type of occupations are taken into account". The OECD also warns that the stock of skills available in England and Northern Ireland is "bound to decline over the next decades unless significant action is taken to improve skills proficiency among people."

John Allan, national chairman of the Federation of Small Businesses, said: "Young people don't have the literacy and numeracy skills to do the job properly. 16- to 24-year-olds need to improve their English and maths and to gain work skills and experience."

Too many UK students start science courses with weak maths skills. The UK House of Lords Science and Technology Committee has called for immediate action to boost student numbers in science, technology, engineering and maths at undergraduate and postgraduate level. The committee's report show that few students study maths beyond GCSE.

Too few students take postgraduate degrees in science, technology, engineering and maths (Stem) subjects. Many Stem undergraduates do not have A-level mathematics.

The Royal Academy of Engineering has estimated that the minimum number of STEM graduates (science, technology, engineering, and mathematics) needed to keep industry fully resourced is around 100,000 per year. Only about 90,000 STEM students graduate annually in the UK - and up to a quarter of them go on to choose non-STEM occupations.

The figures showed that around 70% of biology undergraduates, 38% of chemistry and economics undergraduates and 10% of engineering students did not have A-level maths.

The OECD report states that the quality of the Stem graduates coming out of universities does not meet the requirements of industry and in fact is ultimately not even likely to meet the requirements of academia. It argues that without action, the government risks failing to meet its objective of driving economic growth through education and hi-tech industries.

Semta – the sector skills council for science, engineering and manufacturing technologies – has warned that it was facing a shortfall of 80,000 workers in 2014-15.

As a result, foreigners have taken up 20 per cent of jobs in fields such as oil and gas extraction, aerospace, manufacturing, IT and engineering.

Shortage of Graduates with numeracy skills

Government figures show that almost half the working population of England have only primary school maths skills. 78% of Britons have numeracy below Maths GCSE Grades A* to C standard. Of those, 25% of people have numeracy skills equivalent to the average 9 to 11 year old. According to the British charity National Numeracy, millions of British people struggle to understand a payslip, a train timetable, or pay a household bill. It suggests that poor numeracy has become like a "badge of honour" and that poor numeracy is costing the UK economy £20bn per year.

Most Britons may not be able to understand price labels on pre-packaged food. They may not be able to compare products and services for the best buy or work out a household budget. British supermarkets often exploit peoples' poor maths skills by making ridiculous offers. Here is a recent example: One bottle of Robinson's fruit squash costs £1. The special offer in a supermarket was "Buy two for £2".

The boss of the Morrisons supermarket chain has criticised Britain's educational system claiming many school leavers who turn up at his stores for jobs are no good at maths and can't spell.

Dalton Philips, 45, said he was concerned that UK schools were falling behind those in other countries and failing to teach basic numeracy and literacy skills.

These raise worrying concerns about the long-term problems that could arise in the British economy.

If maths or numbers do not faze you, the good news is that there are professions (science and maths teachers and accountants) where numeracy skills are in high demand particularly in and around London and the south in general.

The UK Needs Teachers

According to the Department for Education (DfE), there are 1.3 million teachers in the UK. Of these 96% have degrees, 75% of them are women and 99% of them are white. The average salary of a secondary school teacher is £38,000 per year, while that of a Head teacher is £62,000.

There are many subjects in which there is a shortage of qualified teachers in the UK. These subjects are

- Design and Technology

- Maths

- Physics

- Chemistry

- Engineering

- Science

According to Prof. John Howson of Oxford Brookes University, the government's new School Direct scheme is recruiting too few trainee teachers in key subjects, like Physics with 75% of places vacant. Prof. Howson analysed acceptances onto School Direct schemes and onto traditional university Post Graduate Diploma in Education (PGCE) courses. He argues that although the scheme was coping well in many of the arts and humanities subjects, it was failing badly to recruit trainee teachers in key Science, Mathematics and Technology subjects.

There was a 9.3% fall in the number of graduates who registered to start secondary school teacher training courses in September 2011. As a result there has been a teacher shortage in the UK. The gap has been filled by temporary teachers who are called Supply Teachers. The number of supply teachers in the UK as a whole rose by over 10% between the years 2012-13. The greatest demand was in London schools where the number of supply teachers rose 41%.

The shortage of maths teachers in the UK is so acute that graduates who take up a maths teaching post at a further education (FE) college in England will be given a "golden hello" of £7,500 by the Department for Business, Innovation and Skills (BIS). The money will be paid in the second year of teaching. This £20m FE maths teacher recruitment drive will also give colleges bonus payments of £20,000 if they recruit a graduate maths teacher.

If you have a university degree from the UK in any one of the subjects mentioned above and if you like school teaching, there are great career opportunities awaiting you.

Those from within the EEA and Switzerland are allowed to use their existing teaching qualifications and do not need to retrain.

Information for teachers who are from outside the EEA and Switzerland

• Teachers from outside the EEA (Overseas Trained Teachers -OTTs) are subject to UK Visa requirements.

• You must be qualified as a teacher overseas. In addition, if you qualified outside the EEA, you will need: a qualification comparable to a UK Bachelor degree, to demonstrate that you meet a standard equivalent to GCSE grade C in mathematics and English, to demonstrate a standard equivalent to a grade C in a science GCSE if you intend to teach primary or key stage 2/3 (ages 7-14).

• UK NARIC can confirm whether your qualifications meet the first two of these criteria. UK NARIC is the national agency responsible for providing information and advice about how qualifications and skills from overseas compare to the UK's national qualification frameworks. You can apply online with NARIC.

• The Education (Specified Work) (England) Regulations 2012 allow teachers trained in a country outside of the UK to teach in state maintained schools and non-maintained special schools in England for up to four years. During this period they must attain QTS (Qualified Teacher Status).

• Teachers who qualified in countries outside the EEA and Switzerland are still subject to the four year rule even if they do not require Home Office permission to work or remain in the UK.

• OTTs either before or shortly after arrival in the UK must check with UK NARIC to establish whether their home qualifications are equivalent to a UK first degree and also to a GCSE grade 'C' in maths and English (and science if the person is a primary teacher).

• Teachers who qualified in Canada, Australia, New Zealand and the United States of America may apply for qualified teacher status without further training or assessment in England.

• The National College for Teaching and Leadership Information Line is 0800 3892500.

NEETs

Youngsters Not in Education, Employment or Training are called Neets. There are about 900,000 young people in the UK classified as being Neet. The Neets suffer depression, rarely leave home, and find it difficult to get back into studying, join apprenticeships, or take up work. There has been a long-term problem with youth unemployment in the UK, particularly for youngsters who have left school with poor qualifications. Things have got worse for them now.

A 2012 study, funded jointly by the Economic and Social Research Council and the UK Commission for Employment and Skills, suggests that the number of jobs in the UK requiring a degree has overtaken the total of posts not needing any qualifications. More than a quarter of jobs are now available only to graduates, the study says.

The study shows a major shift in the job market towards requiring many more skilled workers, as jobs disappear for those without qualifications.

The findings of the Skills and Employment Survey, with the latest figures for 2012, show a marked change in UK employment patterns, with graduate jobs at a record high level and unskilled jobs at a record low.

This is proof of the difficulties facing unqualified and poorly qualified young people entering the job market.

This has led to a skills mismatch between employers being unable to find suitably qualified staff while there are high numbers of unemployed youngsters.

The OECD has argued that increasing the number of graduates and skilled workers will help to drive economic growth and that those without skills will find themselves increasingly marginalised and with poor job prospects.

Although the overall UK unemployment rate has been steadily declining and there are a record number of people in work, levels of long-term unemployment and youth joblessness remain stubbornly high.

It is now accepted in the UK government that skills shortages within the UK are causing joblessness among UK youth. According to British PM David Cameron (speaking in October 2013) migrants "should not be blamed" for coming to Britain to work, and tighter immigration controls alone will not create more opportunities for British workers.

Speaking to workers at the Mini factory near Oxford, Mr Cameron warned of a potential skills gap among British workers that could hurt their prospects and the long-term growth of the British economy. He said of immigrants from Eastern Europe working in UK factories, "You can't blame them. They have got to work hard. They see the jobs, they come over and they do them."

There are jobs requiring skilled workers in the UK, but not all unemployed UK youth are able to make use of these opportunities. Are you a skilled or a professionally qualified person or a UK university graduate wanting to get ahead?

Do UK Employers Like the Work Ethic of Foreigners?

Jamie Oliver is a celebrity chef and television personality in the UK. He runs, among others, a chain of 30 Italian restaurants in the UK and employs hundreds of staff. Talking in August 2013 about his restaurants in the UK he said that all of his restaurants would close immediately if it were not for European immigrants who are prepared to work long hours in hot kitchens. He said European immigrants were "stronger" and "tougher" than many British youngsters.

According to London's Mayor, Boris Johnson, the reason most catering jobs went to people from overseas was because migrants offered better service as well as lower costs. Boris Johnson told the 2013 Conservative party conference that British teenagers were too lazy to do the 'menial' jobs snapped up by immigrant workers which keep the economy moving. He said further that many young Brits view some jobs as too 'menial' for them to accept.

Studies by the UK's Centre for Social Justice in 2011 have shown that many British employers prefer to employ foreigners than British youngsters because of the former's better work ethic. This finding is supported by Ratan Tata, the Chairman of Tata Sons, the holding company of the Tata group, which owns British companies Corus, and Jaguar Land Rover. He expressed concern in the British media at the work ethic of his British workforce. He was comparing them with his companies' Indian workforce back home.

According to British employers, the crucial difference made by foreigners appears to be the willingness to rise to the occasion especially at weekends when the exigencies of work demand such working. The British people do not have a culture of working on weekends and holidays because of work demands.

A 2013 study by the National Institute of Economic and Social Research claimed that British companies choose to employ foreign workers because migrants work harder and are better qualified for many jobs than those born in the UK. The study found that companies were able to become more efficient and could expand their business by hiring skilled foreigners. Researchers interviewed executives from British firms, many of whom complained about the work ethic of young people in the UK. Concerns were raised that UK children leave school with inadequate numerical and maths skills while others are 'poorly equipped for the workplace' and have aspirations which are ill-matched to real opportunities available to them.

The research, which included employer interviews, focus groups and data analysis, also found that British workers accepted the need for skilled migration and have benefited from working alongside migrants.

Lance Batchelor, the chief executive of Dominos Pizza, said he could create 1,000 jobs in the UK – but too many British people do not want the work – being a driver or working in production. He said it was becoming 'harder and harder to hire staff, especially in London and the South East' of England.

The former boss of Marks & Spencer, Sir Stuart Rose, has criticised the work ethic of many British people and said it was wrong to criticise immigrants prepared to work for lower salaries. Sir Stuart said: 'It is up to people to decide whether they want to do the work for the pay that is being offered. If they don't, somebody else is there to do it. What's wrong with that?' He said that Romanians and Bulgarians and other immigrants should not be blamed for coming to the UK if Britons were not prepared to do menial jobs.

It is fair to conclude that many UK employers would prefer employing foreigners in certain professions.

Exams and Hard Work?

The UK is a post-material society. Very few people in the UK live on the edge of survival. British people are able to indulge in their idiosyncrasies, turning away from the pressing needs of survival. The British are generally looking for easy and well-paid jobs. They are good at, and like jobs in, the creative industries, design, and management.

The British generally do not choose jobs like cleaners, shelf-stockers, and care workers. They do not like exams, unsociable hours of work, manual work, and cleaning. Only those with few other options choose professions with these features.

The British want more leisure, not physical hard work. Talk to school students and no one gives the impression that they see exams as an opportunity to prove their ability. They see them just a pain that can't be avoided. GCSE exams are the first time any student in Britain faces serious pressure in their school lives.

On the other hand, in other parts of the world, young people accept exams as a fact of life and a way to get ahead. The opportunities for studious, hardworking and skilled migrants, who are less concerned about leisure, and see exams as a way to proving themselves, are many in the UK.

It is no wonder that UK professional bodies (for e.g. Pharmacist, Optician, Doctor, Nurse, and Accountant) that require the candidate to sit rigorous exams in order to secure membership tend to have a high number of foreigners as members.

The attitude and aspirations of immigrant families has been praised by a schools expert. According to Sir Michael Wilshaw, the head of Ofsted, the school inspection body, migrant parents care more about their children's education than those from white working-class backgrounds. He said on the BBC Today programme that pupils from migrant, black and Asian families were getting more backing at home – and it is helping them outperform their white classmates.

People With Foreign Language Skills

A YouGov poll found that the UK has an alarming shortage of people able to speak the 10 languages vital to its future prosperity and global standing. The poll of more than 4,000 UK adults found that three-quarters (75%) were unable to speak any of the following 10 languages well enough to hold a conversation. These 10 languages are:

1. Spanish

2. Arabic

3. French

4. Mandarin Chinese

5. German

6. Portuguese

7. Italian

8. Russian

9. Turkish

10. Japanese

About 15% of the UK population said they could speak in French but only 6% said the same of their German skills, 4% could converse in Spanish and 2% in Italian.

The British Council states that schools should teach a wider range of languages, with language skills given the same status as the sciences and maths,

Failure to act risks the UK losing out both economically and culturally, the British Council warned.

The authors analysed a range of economic, political, cultural and educational factors to define the languages which "will be of crucial importance for the UK's prosperity, security and influence in the world over the next 20 years."

More and more British companies are doing business with Europe and China. There is a shortage of employees with foreign language skills. Speaker of French and German are in very short supply. There is also a demand for Chinese Cantonese and Chinese Mandarin speakers.

A 2014 study by the CfBT Education Trust and the British Council (the Languages Trends Survey) found that most language teachers in British primary schools had no more than a GCSE in the language. There is a shortage of degree qualified foreign language teachers in British primary schools.

A 2013 study by job search engine Adzuna rated the job of Translator as being one of the top ten jobs in the UK. The reasons being high level of job security, high average salaries and excellent income growth potential of up to 8 times starting salary.

Social Workers

Social workers provide advice and support to vulnerable individuals, families, and those living on the margins of society. They are also responsible for helping them to get access to the services they need to improve their situation and well-being. They usually specialise in working with children and families, or with adult service users.

Prospective social workers need to study for a three-year undergraduate degree or a two-year postgraduate degree in social work that is approved by the Health and Care Professions Council (HCPC). They will also need to pass background checks by the Disclosure and Barring Service (DBS).

Starting salaries range from £19,500 to £25,000 a year. With more experience and responsibility, this can rise to between £26,000 and £40,000.

Due to staff shortages a new fast-track social work training scheme was piloted in Greater London and Greater Manchester from September 2013. It aimed to train 100 graduates (2:1 in any subject) to become social workers, specialising in working with vulnerable children and their families.

The plan was that the scheme would be an intensive work-based programme spread over two years. Trainees were expected to be placed in a local authority, have their training funded and be paid a salary.

More information about social work as a career can be found by typing these phrases in Google:

- British Association of Social Workers (BASW)

- The College of Social Work

Department of Education — Becoming a social worker. Go to www.gov.uk and type in "Step up to social work."

Home Office List of Skills Shortages in the UK

The UK Home Office lists various UK jobs as being in the Skills Shortage list where immigrant workers are welcomed. This means that non-EU migrants having these skills will find it easy to get leave to work in the UK. A quick glance reveals that most of these required skills are either engineering or science-based i.e. they are technical skills.

This list goes into detail and mentions specific occupations, level of specialisation, skill levels and salary that can be expected. The list is updated from time to time. The list broadly indicates that the UK needs:

- engineers of most specialisations

- software and IT professionals

- doctors, nurses, and medical technicians

- geologists and geophysicists

- science teachers

- social workers

- computer graphics experts and animators for the film, television or video games sectors

- ballet and other dancers and choreographers

- musicians who meet the standard required by internationally recognised UK orchestras (including London Symphony Orchestra, London Philharmonic Orchestra, Philharmonia Orchestra and Royal Philharmonic Orchestra

- graphic designers

- welders

- chefs

The full and up to date list is available here:

http://www.ukba.homeoffice.gov.uk/sitecontent/documents/workingintheu k/shortageoccupationlistnov11.pdf

Foreign Entrepreneurs in the UK

The UK is business friendly

The UK was ranked the eighth best country to do business for a ninth consecutive year in 2014, according to an annual survey by the World Bank. The World Bank ranking used metrics such as the time taken to launch and close a business, gain construction permits and pay taxes in a country's largest business city.

According to the Centre for Entrepreneurs, foreign migrant entrepreneurs are behind the creation of one in seven UK companies. Nearly half a million people from 155 countries have settled in the UK and launched businesses. They are twice as entrepreneurial as British-born people of working age with 17.2 per cent having launched their own businesses, compared to 10.4 per cent of those born in the UK. This is despite the extra challenges they face including access to finance and cultural and language barriers. They are on average younger than British entrepreneurs at 44.3 years-old compared to 52.1.The top ten nationalities that account for more than 260,000 businesses in the UK are (in order, highest first)

Irish

Indian

German

American

Chinese

Polish

French

Italian

Pakistani

Nigerian

Most of these migrant-led businesses are set up in London (188,000). This is twenty times the number of such businesses in Birmingham (19,000), the second popular location.

The top 6 places where migrant-led businesses have been set up:

1. London

2. Birmingham

3. Belfast

4. Manchester

5. Reading

6. Cardiff

Other books by the author

The material in the present book *Going to the UK?: Ten Things You Should Know* has offered you some important advice for your UK life. But there are still many more things you could be aware of to maximise the positives of your UK experience. A more detailed book, with answers to over 300 questions typically asked by new migrants to the UK is available:

Complete Guide to Living, Working and Studying in the UK: Preparing You for Life in Britain by *Rajiv Immanuel* (available at all Amazon websites worldwide) is that book. Following the advice in that book could save your life!

Nearly twenty years of living in the UK and several years of research produced that book

It deals with the following subjects:

1. ARRIVAL IN THE UK

2. IMMIGRATION ISSUES

3. ACCOMMODATION AND PROPERTY

4. STUDYING

5. DOMESTIC

6. SCHOOLS AND CHILDREN

7. SHOPPING

8. MOTORING

9. JOBS

10. COMMUNITY

11. MONEY MATTERS

12. MEDIA & ENTERTAINMENT

13. CRIME

14. BRITISH CULTURE

15. IS THE UK THE PLACE FOR YOU?

About The Author: Rajiv Immanuel

Dickens, Hardy, Hopkins, Chaucer, Wordsworth, Shelley, Keats, Shakespeare, Milton, Maugham, Emerson... you name it - we had them all. Works by such authors lined our bookshelves at home in India. Our wealth was mostly in our heads. This was the type of home I was born into in 1965. Apart from being Christians, another way in which we were different from people around us was that we spoke English at home. In India, that was unusual.

After a degree in Economics in 1982, I added an MBA in 1985. I worked for a while as a Civil Servant in India. I soon got bored with pushing files. In 1995 I arrived at Reading University, UK, to study for a Postgraduate degree in Economics. The scholarship I came on is listed in this book. I learnt a lot about UK university life.

As the years passed in the UK, our roots in the UK were strengthened. Both our children were born here in the UK. We realised how much we loved this country and with the Home Office's co-operation decided to make the UK our home.

Meanwhile, I had found my métier in life: to be a writer. Since then I have been a professional observer of life in the UK.

While I have a great regard for this land, I am also aware that like any country there are problems here too.

I am an INFP. It is one of 16 personality types derived from the MBTI (Myers-Briggs Type Indicator). Those who belong to this personality type get a great deal of satisfaction from helping others grow and develop. My life's mission is to write books that help other migrants after me understand this country, make the most of opportunities here, contribute to UK society, and avoid nasty surprises. In short: to prepare new migrants for UK life.

My story is here on Amazon: *The God of All Things: A story of divine intervention*

I hope you find my books helpful and enjoyable. Best wishes for your UK life. Please leave a review. Thanks.

Rajiv Immanuel.